Hot Business

The Evolution of Hot Business

Please refer to: Sit on a Hot Pot Volumes 1 and 2 for the total story and all courses: Hot Tennis/Hot Business/Hot Education/Hot Presentations

By Marshal McMahon

Copy right © 2018

ISBN 9781798786581

Disclaimer

The courses presented in this document are presented as examples of the courses presented over many years. It is essential that a thorough analysis of the client be undertaken before any implementation of these courses.

Table of Contents

The Evolution of Hot Business iv

The Evolution of Hot Business and Maxperformance 11

The cunning guy came to the next tennis session with a master plan. ... 14

The corporate work was threatening to become a major part of my business.. 20

Around this time, we moved to a capital city in Australia. 23

He had a vision that I could do well in Banking and Finance recruitment. 27

Maxperformance for banking and finance was beginning. 29

For the last few years, my banking and finance clients had realised that I could build their businesses even from outside their firm. 34

My contract started with the banking and finance firm. 36

Another major company heard of the success 40

There were 3 financial institutions discussing contracts with me for Maxperformance services... 46

I was asked to start with the research analysts. 50

HOT BUSINESS 54

HOT RESEARCH/MARKETING 54

MORE BONUSES FOR BUSINESS PERSONS, RESEARCHERS, MARKETERS 56

The following Hot Business Course uses the example of Banking and Finance Research Analysts and Dealers and Corporate Advisers. The Hot Business principles apply to all businesses... 57

Who are the clients of the Research Department / Research Analysts ? 58

Definition of Hot Research/Calling/Business 60

THE A – Z OF HOT CALLING 68

HOT RESEARCH/CALLING/BUSINESS VERSUS COLD
RESEARCH/CALLING/BUSINESS 72

COLD RESEARCH / CALLING 76

Relationship Orientation 81

Rapport 82

SELLING SOLUTIONS TO CUSTOMERS 84

GENERATION OF CORPORATE OPPORTUNITIES 100

THE A – Z OF HOT CALLING/MARKETING 102

How to develop a really superb case for the customer to adopt your solution
.... 121

ARISTOTLE'S CATEGORIES OF REALITY = SUPERB ANALYSIS 122

OPEN-ENDED QUESTIONS 125

MAIN ARGUMENTATION AND FALLBACK POSITIONS 136

DEVELOP THE CUSTOMER'S PERSONAL COMMITMENT TO THE PURCHASE
OF THE SOLUTION 139

THE ACTUAL APPROACH 143

TO THE CUSTOMER 143

PROPOSITIONS TO ACTION 150

PRESENTATIONS 161

CUSTOMER DATABASES 163

Hot Research – Hot Calling – 168

Hot Business Results 168

After 5 years at the bank, an opportunity arose to be part of a product
development business 175

Lesson 1: big companies are only too happy to talk with you and say they want the product. 177

Engineering Departments 179

Our company then developed a retrofit kit which worked on most market products. 185

The Evolution of Hot Business and Maxperformance

Hot Business is set in the context of the evolution of my life.

The Hot Business Course is part of the evolution and has been a major part of my business career.

After the public service career, I was lucky enough to coach some brilliant people.

I was lucky enough to have a range of brilliant clients covering the fields of science, business leadership, political leadership etc.

One business leader was a client for about 8 years.

He realised that the principles of Maxperformance were applicable to many areas of life.

He told me that he had adapted my Maxperformance principles to his career with success.

He was convinced that I had a lot more to give to the world than just tennis coaching.

I discussed the job with him till he finally prevailed

There was a project in a senior political office.

A long term senior public service officer was in danger of losing her position.

I had 3 weeks to turn around her performance or the senior politician would let her go.

I could fit in the contract with my usual work load.

Would be interesting indeed.

On the day, I started the project like any philosophical, logical analysis with the collection of data.

I met nearly all people in the office.

Interviewing them individually with the use of open ended questions around Aristotle's categories of reality:

- *Essence*
- *Quality*
- *Quantity*
- *Time*
- *Location*

Every question starting with one of the following:

- *How*
- *When*
- *Where*
- *Why*
- *What*
- *Which*

The promise to all interviewees was that the final report would be on an anonymous basis.

With that promise, people are prepared to provide volumes of important data for analysis.

By logically analysing the comprehensive data collection, clear action plans are formed to solve the client's problems.

I presented the analysis and action plan to the client who then authorised the implementation of the action plan.

I worked for a few days with the target officer.

The officer involved, quickly saw the problems and the solutions necessary.

I always work with the target to implement the necessary changes for all round success.

Changes are automated with one to 2 successful repetitions, so change is rapid and results are rapid.

The office was humming within 1-2 weeks.

The client was most appreciative and the target went from strength to strength.

My very senior tennis client who had prompted me to expand my business model to include the corporate world was happy with the whole project.

The cunning guy came to the next tennis session with a master plan.

You know how to fix tennis elbow and maximise muscle movement and efficiency so I have a special project in mind for you.

What's that?

You know how big a problem RSI for typists in the public service is.

Yep.

You know how to fix it don't you.

Yes.

RSI is costing the Government a fortune and a lot of people long term misery.

I would like you to try to fix the problem by working with 5-6 of the worst effected typists.

I said no way.

I may be insured for tennis coaching but I am not a doctor with the appropriate insurance coverage for this project.

If you cover me with insurance, I will take on the project.

How long would it take to fix each case?

Maybe 5 minutes.

But we have the best specialists in the field working on the problem.

Some cases have been under their treatment for up to 5 years with multiple operations and castes to enable them just to live without too much pain.

I suggested that with my maximum performance skills I would stop working on the case if I had not fixed the problem within 5 minutes.

He suggested that he would be back with me in a few days.

He called a few days later.

Would I agree to appear before a panel of 6-7 doctors/specialists for examination.

If I passed their examination I would be covered by insurance.

OK.

On the day, I entered a room and sat in a chair with an arc of top specialists in front of me.

Off we went.

What do you think is the cause of the RSI problem.

Well, before I answer, I would be keen to hear from each of you what you think is the cause of the massive RSI problem.

They were keen to offer their expertise.

Quite a few thought that there was no physical problem at all – it was all psychological.

Basically, the poor RSI suffers just wanted an easy life on compensation.

Others thought it was some sort of complex physical issue requiring various surgeries and immobilisation of limbs.

I boldly suggested that none of the answers was correct.

Well what is the answer.

The co-contraction of opposing muscle lines and the constant loading of the extensor muscles.

The fundamental issue was that the new ergonometric mould for typists was a disaster.

The way typists were told to hover their fingers above the new sensitive electronic key boards was a biomechanical disaster.

The whole efficient seated position for typists was designed to cause pain to the extensor in particular.

The extensor is a muscle type that is brilliant at strike release but a disaster at constant holding such as hovering above a key board.

The seated mould was an overall disaster for many areas of the body.

I will not go into the details of the biomechanics here or it will be just too boring.

The panel of specialists seemed to agree that there may be a logic to my potential solution.

They would think about it and let me know about whether I would be engaged and covered by insurance.

They wanted to know how I would conduct a case.

I said that I would conduct a simple muscle test at the beginning to make sure the muscles in the arm where good.

Then without any physical contact, I would:

1. *clear their locked up thinking processes*
2. *show them how the primary muscle lines worked for typing*
3. *work in reality on any other problems they had such as cooking or peeling potatoes etc*
4. *have them typing and cooking even if their forearms were in plaster casts on the spot*
5. *all work done in their home with the family present*
6. *recommendation that they attend for work asap*

A few days later, the panel asked me to take on 5-6 cases with full insurance cover.

Agreed.

I turned up at the family home of the first case.

She had not typed for several years but dearly wanted to get back to the job she loved.

She also was unhappy at home because she could no longer cook due to the pain in her arms.

I checked her muscles and they were working well – no pain in the test.

I questioned her to determine:

- **how confused her brain was**
- **by the conflict between the overriding moulded learning for typing efficiently on the new touch sensitive key boards and**
- **the natural movement of the complex activity cells in the spinal cord**

Using some trick question and answer techniques, the typist and I were able to return her body to natural painless movement.

She had a typewriter there for the session.

She said can I type now.

Sure can.

Type any way you like.

You were a top typist for many years so just do the same again.

Strike release.

Just like typing with the old machines.

She sat down and typed painlessly and fast.

No pain at all.

Does this mean I can ask for my job back tomorrow.

Sure thing.

She turned up for assessment the next morning.

They cut the plaster off and she went back to work.

Everyone was happy.

What about cooking.

We went to the kitchen, we went through which muscles were needed for cooking and away she went.

If I remember correctly, there were tears of joy.

Life was returning to natural.

I recommended that she never again type according to the evil efficient mould.

Slump slob and relax.

Hammer the key board of the type writer – whatever works for you.

Strike release and enjoy life.

The other test cases went well as well.

Word spread rapidly that the efficient ergonometric typing mould for the new key boards caused pain.

Relaxed and natural was the best.

It was not long before RSI for typists seemed to become a non-issue.

The corporate work was threatening to become a major part of my business.

At this time, my business was also thinking of ways of maximising the efficiency of tennis racquet stringing.

The details of this racquet stringing analysis seem minor.

The major lessons for me in this early racquet stringing project were learning:

- trust is learnt over time
- never trust anyone in business
- trust has to be earned
- relationship is a major factor in business
- thorough preparation assists success
- clear presentations work
- money is seen as all powerful
- do not spend money you do not have
- check to see if someone else has already tried your idea
- you will probably find that the idea has been tried before
- assess whether your idea is worth proceeding with
- think about keeping your knowledge as a trade secret rather than patenting
- small and large firms are tricky
- large firms with money will drag out negotiations till you run low or out of money
- near the end of your finances the large firms will offer you a pittance for the lot
- avoid law suits unless you have massive finances greater than the company you wish to fight in court
- look after your health and happiness first
- look after your family first
- stop the project at the limit of your finances
- never borrow to continue a project
- keep a balance in your life
- never sacrifice your life for a project
- there is always something else to do in life after the end of your dream project

Some entrepreneurs and financiers are rock solid.

Others put on a great show but can vanish the moment their own business is in trouble.

You will usually receive a call from the financier's lawyer rather than the financier in trouble.

The lawyer advises you in plain language the project is over as of this call and if you wish to go further see you in court.

Move on.

You will be glad to be free of the troubled financier so lightly.

If the meetings with a financier involve lavish dinners with $1000 bottles of wine, beware.

Suggest moving on.

Make sure the potential financier can afford to dump the amount required for your project into the sea without worry.

Balanced happy normal people make the best financiers.

If there is good rapport between the parties from the first meeting, there is a chance of success.

If not forget it.

It never gets better.

Around this time, we moved to a capital city in Australia.

The tennis business as a major income earner took a back seat.

I would only coach top players now as per European experience.

The Maxperformance business was difficult to start in the capital city.

Most businesses could not understand that logical analysis and knowledge of how humans work would lead to increased profitability.

Eventually, an executive recruitment firm offered to give me a chance to learn their business.

The boss of the firm thought that my skills would be good at marketing candidates to clients as I could understand exactly what the client required in their business and I could match the best people to that position.

And communicate this clearly to the client.

As a good chap, I followed the boss' words of experience and wisdom as best I could.

Marshal McMahon

The boss was strict.

If you did not follow the instructions and you also failed to bring in profit, you would be called into the relatively sound proof office and blasted from pillar to post with real Aussie language.

If that happened to you a few times, you went.

Several of us had started in the one intake.

The others were all covering their costs but were blasted from pillar to post on a regular basis.

A few of them left.

I had not been called in as yet.

But I knew that my turn would come.

Would be real fun.

There was a group of long term employees of the firm who never got into trouble.

So I would regularly seek their advice on whether to put forward a candidate.

The usual advice was not to.

I rarely could understand their logic.

Anyway, one day I had a top accountant to put forward to a firm so I asked the long termers for advice.

No. Candidate is totally unsuited.

So I was preparing to shelve the idea.

Suddenly, I became conscious that a volcano was heating up right behind me.

So I turned to the volcano and said: I will still be putting the candidate forward.

The volcano quietly said whose business is this yours or theirs.

Stayed with me forever after.

RUN YOUR OWN BUSINESS

Do not automatically follow the advice of others.

Take advice into account but always run your own business.

So I rang up this firm who did not even have a published vacancy for an accountant and put forward a case for this candidate being a valuable asset for their business and a profit centre as he had direct experience in South East Asia in a similar firm.

I can still remember this candidate as it was the first time that I had met anyone where the surname was 2 consonants.

This would also be his first job as an accountant in Australia.

I asked the company if they would like to interview him at 10am tomorrow morning.

Please.

The candidate got the job.

He was with the firm for years and became the company secretary/chief finance officer.

The company was happy the candidate was happy.

My boss was happy.

Marshal McMahon

I was happy.

My boss called me in.

He had a vision that I could do well in Banking and Finance recruitment.

I took on the sector.

Plus for the first time, I decided to use my Maxperformance skills in dealing with the client and the applicants.

I blended my Maxperformance skills with my boss' skills, especially the proposition to action.

My income rocketed from that time.

I would logically analyse the bank or finance company then analyse my candidates for logical relevance to the client and work out how the client would make profit from hiring my candidate.

I would contact the client discuss the candidate and ask when they would like to interview the candidate.

By thorough preparation of an overall business case, my strike rate of placements was high.

My boss was a happy man indeed.

I was a happy man indeed.

My clients became happier and happier.

I only had 2-3 clients.

I serviced their business needs.

They involved me more and more in their businesses.

Sometimes I was able to build a business case for expansion into new areas of profitability.

Maxperformance for banking and finance was beginning.

Word was spreading through the executive recruitment world of my success in banking and finance.

I received a headhunt from an international banking and finance recruitment company for a meeting.

I said that I was happy where I was.

Then they mentioned the package they were offering me to start a senior banking and finance business in Australia.

What time would suit you for a meeting.

The meeting went well.

The plan was to build a banking and finance recruitment firm from scratch in conjunction with another recruiter.

I accepted the project and off we went.

We found an office in the banking and finance sector of the city, designed the interior, recruited some executive recruiters, trained them in Maxperformance principles and launched the business with a marketing event.

Many banking and finance senior executives attended.

A good time was had by all.

The businesses understood that we were interested in their business functional proficiency, profitability and prospects.

Within 1 year we were a highly profitable business.

We were one of the most profitable business arms of the international recruitment firm.

That year the international recruitment firm held the global conference in our city.

I was asked to open the conference on how to maximise business using Maxperformance skills.

OK.

But it won't be a 40 minute lecture.

I never do lectures.

It would be a discussion group for the 600 international attendees.

We would be addressing their issues in real time using Maxperformance skills.

The conference opened.

To my surprise, I was awarded the global prize for the most profitable business centre globally.

There were 3 morning lecturers on the first morning of the conference.

I started my lecture with the announcement that it would be a discussion group solving real business issues.

Basically, my role was of education.

I hate teachers and lecturers.

They tend to implode information into one.

An educator leads it out of the person.

Educo = I lead out of

Dons at Oxford are educators

Buddhist leaders are educators as far as I can see.

The ancient Greek philosophers were educators.

The conference caught fire.

The education program was popular.

Attendees were keen to air their problems because other people were able to offer action plans to solve their problems.

At the end of the 40 minutes, I started to thank everyone and move off the stage.

The moderator stepped forwards and said to me that the next 2 lecturers preferred to continue with the discussion session for the next 2 hours.

The hall voted to continue this valuable time period.

So I stayed on for the next 2 hours.

The education process was a success.

Real problems were solved for many people.

At the lunch break the head of the international firm came over to me and shook my hand.

He insisted that I never leave the firm.

Soon after that conference the head of Australia died.

The replacement head was a hatchet man from overseas.

The old boss was brilliant at building business.

The hatchet man was brilliant at destroying business.

The writing was on the wall for all in the Australian company.

There were difficult economic times.

No better time to gain market share and then boom in the good times.

The hatchet men of the world leave businesses in a crippled state.

The hatchet idea is to rebuild after the destruction.

Meanwhile, the hatchet man has destroyed the established businesses.

No clients want to do business with firms that abandon them in their times of need.

My division was still profitable.

But every day I had to argue that our business should be left as is.

The clients needed us more and more.

It was tough resisting a determined hatchet man.

At some point, I held a meeting with my fellow workers who were keen to discuss the situation.

We operated in an open management style so my fellow workers understood what was happening.

We all agreed that if an opportunity arose for them to find other employment they would.

One by one they left.

The hatchet man was thrilled.

His business was shrinking to zero.

For the last few years, my banking and finance clients had realised that I could build their businesses even from outside their firm.

I understood the logic of business.

The clients had been suggesting that I should join them and help build their businesses.

Finally, one client rang and offered me a contract starting in a few days time.

I met them and signed the contract.

Then told my happy hatchet man.

Hot Business

If the business was disappearing he was happy.

One of my fellow workers stayed on buoyed by the hatchet man's promise to build the business around him.

Good luck.

He was the only one left.

He was dismissed by the hatchet man not long after.

My contract started with the banking and finance firm.

Maximum performance principles were now being applied to the world of banking and finance.

This first contract involved:

- **collection of data about the client service division**
- **logical analysis of the data**
- **production of logical action plans to enhance the budgetary elements, functional proficiency and prospects of the division**

The collection of data was on a guaranteed confidential basis.

There was plenty of data.

The report collected all the raw data on this confidential basis.

The client was astonished by the views expressed by the employees of the division.

There was total anonymity so no one was embarrassed or victimised.

I assisted in the initial implementation of the action plan.

Soon the contract was over.

Client was happy.

Their clients were happy.

Next client wanted the whole organisation overhauled.

The project was to analyse the whole company and hopefully address some major problems such as a staff turnover of around 93% per annum.

The cost to the company was high.

I suggested that the data collection would take about 3-4 days, the analysis and solutions about 1 week and implementation several months.

This was an international firm that suffered from this problem worldwide.

Some of the famous management consultancies of the world had been engaged to solve the problems.

Cost a lot.

Seemed to still be a problem.

I was given permission to collect data on an anonymous basis across all 13 or so floors and at nearly all levels of the company.

All the employees were cooperative.

I collected the data in about 3-4 days and began the analysis.

There was a major trend in the data.

The company was heavily computerised in its processes.

Level 1 of the building:

- **entered the data into a computer system**
- **processed the data on that floor's systems**
- **printed out the data**
- **took the data the next floor up**

Where the whole process was repeated on each floor.

The graduates on each floor were bored stupid.

Soon left for more full filling jobs elsewhere.

To keep the firm in functioning order, there was a large pool of new graduates being inaugurated at all times.

Using logic I soon worked out that the numbers of employees could be reduced from around 900 to 80 in less than 12 months.

I worked out the logic steps for a programmer to link the computers on each floor.

There would be no printing out.

I showed the logic steps to one of the programmers at the client.

He confirmed the logic and assured that the programming was relatively easy.

I presented my report to the client.

The client was slightly stunned.

There was a certain element of incredulity.

The report was sent to the overseas head office.

My part in the contract was cancelled.

The head office took over.

The program would be tried at my client.

Within a year the numbers were around 80.

I believe the program then went worldwide.

The next year, head office upgraded the program and the numbers went even lower.

Profit for the company.

Good news.

Another major company heard of the success.

I was asked to analyse their company.

Great contract: analysing back offices linked to analysts, dealers and traders and corporate areas.

This was fun.

The data collection was easy and fun.

Everyone was cooperative.

I analysed the data and wrote the report on how to maximise the profitability of the company.

The client liked the report.

I was asked to maximise the strike rate of the dealers first.

This would lead to increased functional proficiency, more deals with clients and higher profitability.

I analysed the skill base of the whole desk and of each dealer.

Then I established the logic of how to maximise the presentation of the product to the client by the dealer.

The dealer was to summarise the call to the client into a major premise with 3 dot point reasons to deal.

Then the big one.

The proposition to action.

If you do the initial work and forget the proposition to action you will lose 90% of the deals.

The senior dealers picked this up quickly.

Quite a few senior dealers were already so skilled in these areas, increased profit soon followed.

The more junior dealers quickly took up the processes.

Results soon came.

The process was proving itself.

This was the beginning of my Hot Business Course.

This course will follow this client experience.

The research division was next.

All analysts were polite and cooperative.

Instead of writing huge academic reports on companies, my idea and that of the institutional clients was that the report should present the buy or sell recommendation in the top one third of the front page.

In fact the Report title on the front cover should really be the essence of the report.

The report should start with a major premise on buying or selling the company stock supported by 3 dot point reasons to buy or sell.

If the analyst was talking to the client a proposition to action should be included.

If the client wanted to transact, the client could be transferred to a dealer.

The details of the business process will be in Hot Research to follow soon.

One of the major income earners I could see from the research was corporate advisory or corporate actions such as Mergers and Acquisitions.

The idea was to assist the analysts to become conscious of corporate activity and pass it over the wall of silence to the corporate division.

The corporate division took over from there.

The analysts played no part in corporate activity.

Unless they moved over the other side of the wall for the project or even permanently for some.

My client earned more share of the client investment money according to the quality, usability and ranking of the research analysts.

The research department was already well ranked.

But more analysts climbed the client panel ranking using the new processes.

Institutional clients demanded short and sweet research but some analysts think volume is the key.

If so I suggested that I did not care how much they wrote as long as the first one third of the of the first page of the research paper was according to the summary process.

In fact, the clients would tell me that the title of the research paper on the front cover was important in making them pull the

paper out of a pile of hundreds that landed on their desk every day.

Some institutions showed me what they did each morning.

They would pull the dust bin over to the side of their desk.

Pile the research papers from all the stock broking companies into one high pile on the desk above the bin.

Then looking only at the title on the front page, they would either put the paper on the desk for further examination or throw the paper into the bin.

The vast majority of papers went into the bin without ever being opened.

Then the fund manager opened the few research papers on the desk.

If the major premise interested them they kept the paper for reading or threw it in the bin if there was no summary or the summary did not interest them.

Many thousands of dollars of research was never opened.

Next I worked in the corporate division.

Collecting the data was most interesting.

This division was in relative turmoil.

There were hidden agendas and power plays in this division.

It did not take me long to realise that one person in particular was keen on replacing the leader with himself.

I did not write this in my report.

However, I did advise my corporate client that there was a plot to replace him by X.

He did not believe me.

Especially, as X was not really successful at corporate action.

I advised that even so he was constantly back biting and moving at high levels to undermine the division so he could take over and make a positive difference.

I did agree that X would never be successful.

But we disagreed about whether his undermining would work at high levels.

In the long term, the undermining at high levels worked unfortunately.

But as predicted, the senior management woke up and the revolutionary was dismissed.

But in the meantime, the corporate division started kicking goals and goals.

The processes of making the heading powerful and the first one third of page 1 of the corporate report with a proposition to action was working.

Deals were being made.

There were spot fires breaking out all the time within the division and the boss was distracted at times firefighting.

But progress was always being made.

I assisted in the fire fighting.

But X was keen on the revolution.

Hot Business

My contract was coming to an end.

There were 3 financial institutions discussing contracts with me for Maxperformance services.

I was down the track with 2 of them when I went for the interview with the third.

The interview was going well.

The job was to turn around a relatively unprofitable stockbroking and corporate advisory division of a merchant bank.

After about 30-60 minutes, it was clear that there was a strong synergy between the senior executive and my ideas.

He had heard good things about Maxperformance in the market place.

The merchant bank had just had one of the biggest accounting firms conduct a contract to get the division to profit.

Jobs had been slashed, budgets cut.

All to no end.

I advised that I would finish the interviews with the other financial institutions and let him know where I stood.

He said sorry.

But you are not leaving this room till you sign on the dotted line.

What do you want?

I thought of my highest number and as confidently as possible gave him the number.

Sure.

Anything else.

Now I knew I had started too low.

So I said and the bonus structure of course.

Sorry.

We do not give bonuses to contractors.

I now thought I had time to finish all my discussions.

But in your case we will make an exception.

The deal was that I would start at the same time as the new MD of the division and turn the division to profit.

No worrles.

I signed on the bottom line.

Great challenge.

But before I went he said: the name of your Maxperformance course is just not good enough for an expert who thinks he is good at marketing.

The stockbrokers need a catchy name.

HOT CALLING!

Excellent.

Start tomorrow at 7am.

The contract was for around 6 months.

When the time came, neither party even thought about it.

On we went for nearly 5 years.

We were having fun and making profit for our clients and the merchant bank.

I conducted my usual data collection and observation and wrote a report on the state of play.

Basically, sales and client development was still in the red wine lunch era.

Fill the client with a top lunch and lots of wine and you could expect an order for a share transaction.

Meanwhile, the best ranked broker was all about demonstrating to the client:

- *how much profit the client could make from their proposals*
- *how easy they were to use for the client*
- *how the client prospects would be in the short, medium and long term.*

My report went all the way to the top of the bank.

I was called in.

I suggested that by upgrading the sales and marketing techniques of the division to top level, the clients would soon reward us with increased profitability and market share.

I was asked to start with the research analysts.

The analysts were in the land of the major work – 100 pages minimum.

I surveyed the institutional clients to see what they wanted.

I already knew from my other surveys they wanted:

- **a strong heading for the report**
- **the major premise and 3 supporting dot points at the top of the front page**
- **1-3 pages in total**

Any longer than that and they did not read them.

Also they had little respect for my client's work and we would have to produce outstandingly logical analysis to make it onto their client list – especially the top 10 where you could actually start making some money in commissions.

The report was presented to the whole division.

The analysts seemed reasonably ok with changing.

Many of the dealers/sales desk were strongly arguing for the red wine lunch technique.

I was asked many times if there were any staff I think should be fired.

I do not use the word.

I was convinced that each person would make it to the top 3 analysts or dealers.

I was also convinced that there was great potential to initiate corporate deals from the research while obeying all the appropriate legal requirements.

So I created   HOT RESEARCH.

A few days later, all the analysts gathered in the one room for HOT RESEARCH.

The revolution was starting.

At this point, I will present HOT RESEARCH for your consideration.

PLEASE NOTE:

HOT RESEARCH: A COURSE FOR ANALYSTS

HOT CALLING: A COURSE FOR SALES REPRESENTATIVES OR DEALERS

HOT BUSINESS: A COURSE FOR CORPORATE FINANCE SPECIALISTS

ALL THESE COURSES ARE SIMILAR TO A LARGE EXTENT SO I AM ONLY PRESENTING HOT RESEARCH HERE.

OTHERWISE THE READER WOULD FIND THE COURSES A REPETITIVE PAIN.

THE PRINCIPLES ARE ALL THE SAME.

Marshal McMahon

HOT BUSINESS

HOT RESEARCH/MARKETING

GUIDE

TO

HOT BUSINESS –
HOT RESEARCH –
HOT MARKETING

MORE BONUSES FOR BUSINESS PERSONS, RESEARCHERS, MARKETERS

The following Hot Business Course uses the example of Banking and Finance Research Analysts and Dealers and Corporate Advisers. The Hot Business principles apply to all businesses

Marshal McMahon

Who are the clients of the Research Department / Research Analysts ?

Answer:

INSTITUTIONAL FUND MANAGERS

SALES SPECIALISTS

CORPORATE ADVISORS

COMPANY CEO'S, CFO'S ETC

Definition of Hot

Research/Calling/Business

HOT RESEARCH/CALLING/BUSINESS

IS

MAXIMISING

THE PROFITABILITY

FUNCTIONAL PROFICIENCY

(ADMINISTRATIVE

PROCESSES)

AND

PROSPECTS

OF THE CUSTOMER

HOT RESEARCH/MARKETING/BUSINESS

IS

DEMONSTRATING

TOTAL DEDICATION

TO THE

FUNDAMENTAL

BUSINESS NEEDS OF YOUR

CUSTOMER

AND

YOUR CUSTOMERS'

CUSTOMERS

YOU ENJOY YOUR WORK MORE

MAKE MORE MONEY AND

THE CUSTOMERS LOVE YOU

THE STRONGEST FORM

OF MARKETING/BUSINESS POSSIBLE

YOU HAVE ESTABLISHED

YOURSELF

ABOVE THE REST OF THE

MARKETPLACE

YOU WILL BEAT YOUR COMPETITORS AND IT'S EASY

YOUR SUCCESS AND

FUTURE ARE ASSURED

YOUR STRIKE RATE IS

UP AND CONTINUES TO RISE

GUIDE TO HOT CALLING

TABLE OF CONTENTS

Prelude

- ® Aim of Research Group

    (Hot Research/ Calling versus Cold Research/Calling)

- ® Selling Solutions to Customers

- ® Commercial Research

- ® Additional Factors Ensuring Closure of the Deal

- ® Proposition to Action

- ® Generation of Corporate Opportunities

THE A – Z OF HOT CALLING

A   Selling or Marketing to a particular customer

B   Analysing the effects of your solutions on the needs of your customers

The SCHEMA:

BUDGET-FUNCTION-PROSPECTS

How to deal with vague feelings

Summary schema

C   Aids for the thorough development of the previous schema. Including:

UNIVERSAL ANALYTICAL SYSTEM

(Aristotle)

OPEN – ENDED QUESTIONS

D   Logical argumentation and fall-back positions. Practical example of questioning processes.

E   Develop the Customer's personal commitment to the purchase of the solution.

F   The actual approach to the Customer

G   Propositions – Close the deal – examples

H   Presentations –

   The winning presentation

7 Customer databases

PRELUDE

HOT

RESEARCH/CALLING/BUSINESS

VERSUS COLD

RESEARCH/CALLING/BUSINESS

DESTROYING THE MYTH

AIM OF RESEARCH/SALES TEAM

The aim of all marketing and selling by the Research Team is to make profit through the conclusion of a business deal by supplying successful solutions to your established or targeted customer base.

Your central focus and total determination from the beginning to the end of the deal, is the successful conclusion of the business deal with the customer.

PROFIT THROUGH THE CLOSURE OF CUSTOMER DEALS

INCREASING YOUR STRIKE RATE OF CLOSURES

INCREASING SALES OF SOLUTIONS

Maximisation of deal closures occurs when the needs of the customers are clearly established and the customer is convinced by the salesperson that the solutions on offer will satisfy those needs and maximize the relationship between the customer and the customer's customer.

COLD RESEARCH / CALLING

Often the ability to cold call is regarded highly by some as the secret to successful salesmanship and marketing.

Simply contact a company.

Tell the customer how wonderful, successful and highly rated your own company's solutions and services are.

The customer is bound to be so impressed that the orders will follow in due course.

ALL THE BEST !

Certainly, some orders will follow.

However, this cold calling approach ignores the needs of the customer and the customer's customer.

So many deals will be lost and many doors will slam in your face.

ARGUMENT FROM AUTHORITY

ARGUMENTUM AD HOMINEM OR "MAN TO MAN ARGUMENT"

This cold calling approach uses the "argument from authority" and the "argumentum ad hominem" or the "man to man argument".

These are the two weakest forms of argumentation available to win the case. Many deals will be lost.

<u>There is a principle in law, "what is freely asserted can be freely denied."</u>

The customer can simply deny whatever is said when this form of cold calling is used.

The customer wants to hear your solutions to their problems, not how great you think you are.

Consequently, the employee is usually instinctively uncomfortable with using the cold calling approach as part of the sales technique.

Rightly so !

The cold call wastes the customer's valuable time.

In fact, you might not even get into see the customer.

THE CUSTOMER REACTS COOLLY

The cold caller generally feels embarrassed and becomes reluctant to continue in sales.

STRIKE RATES SUFFER

Marshal McMahon

COLD CALLING IS AN INSULT TO THE CLIENT

Relationship Orientation

For many marketers and salespersons establishing a FRIENDLY relationship with a customer is the main purpose of the daily business routine.

Some sales will flow from the relationship.

However, the strike rate for the salesperson will usually be average, especially in difficult market and economic conditions.

Relationship orientation must be linked with a full business approach to be effective.

The customer's business needs are far more important than personal matters.

Rapport

Establishing rapport with the customer is an essential part of the business transaction and will ensure a profitable relationship with the customer.

HOT RESEARCH / CALLING is a fully professional method of selling and marketing which gains the business respect of the customer towards you and your company

Results increase and all parties profit

SELLING SOLUTIONS TO

CUSTOMERS

What makes sure a customer takes your solution ?

YOUR SOLUTION MUST ENHANCE YOUR CUSTOMER IN THE EYES OF THE CUSTOMER'S CUSTOMERS.

If the selling technique by your company only demonstrates the benefits to the customer on the plane of your company to customer, there is much less chance of the customer wishing to take up the offer.

When selling or designing solutions for sale consider the whole market situation.

Your sales will flow and increase.

CONCENTRATE ON THIS RELATIONSHIP

THE CUSTOMER AND THE CUSTOMER'S CUSTOMER

DEALS WILL FLOW

Technical information applies generally only to the relationship between your company and the Customer.

Technical information as the major thrust of a sale will result in a lower strike rate.

THE SECRET OF MARKETING SUCCESS IN THIS AND MANY CASES IS TO BE SEEN TO BE ENHANCING THE CUSTOMER IN THE EYES OF THEIR PAYING CUSTOMERS AND INVESTORS.

COMMERCIAL RESEARCH A SOLUTION TO A DIFFICULT MARKETING PROBLEM

The Research Team has a difficult marketing job. Your markets are multiple with varying needs:

INSTITUTIONAL FUND MANAGERS

INTERNAL SALES SPECIALISTS

& CORPORATE ADVISORS

The Research Team can either prepare at least 3 different versions of the business proposal or create one business proposal to satisfy the needs of the various markets.

Corporate proposals may be specialised.

Whether the business proposal is written or verbal, 1 or 400 pages long, the format which will satisfy the needs of all the clients is described as follows:

PAGE 1 – For Institutional Fund Managers, Internal Sales Specialists, Corporate Advisors

The first half of Page 1 will contain:

1) The logical argument necessary to demand a YES or NO answer to the business proposal you are presenting, and

2) The proposition to action, which will directly evoke the YES or NO authorization from the client to proceed with the implementation of the portfolio recommendations.

THE FOLLOWING 1 OR MORE PAGES – FOR FOLLOW UP ACTION

The following 1 or 400 pages will contain detailed information and argumentation reinforcing the main logical argumentation and proposition to action on the first half of page 1.

The information pages will cover the benefits of the products being discussed under the headings of:

BUDGET

FUNCTION

PROSPECTS

Marshal McMahon

PAGE 1

OF A BUSINESS PROPOSAL

DECISION MAKING FORMAT FOR INSTITUTIONAL FUND MANAGERS, INTERNAL SALES SPECIALISTS, CORPORATE ADVISORS ⟶	LOGICAL ARGUMENTATION Invest $2,000,000 in product T Reasons 1, 2 and 3 Sell $1,000,000 of rival A Reason 1 Sell $500,000 of rival B Reason 1 and Sell $500,000 or rival C Reason 1
	PROPOSITION TO ACTION
FOLLOW UP ANALYSIS ⟶	INFORMATION BACKING LOGICAL ARGUMENTATION PLUS

THOROUGH
FOLLOW UP ⟶
ANALYSIS ON

PROPOSITION TO ACTION
BUDGET FUNCTION AND PROSPECTS

ADDITIONAL FACTORS ENSURING THE CLOSURE OF THE DEAL

THE CUSTOMER WORKS FOR YOU

The extra, personal factors which facilitate a favourable decision by the customer are:

REMUNERATION

FUNCTIONAL SATISFACTION

PROSPECTS

LOCATION

As these apply to the decision maker.

One of these factors will be a primary motivator for the customer.

Determine which one by subtle questioning and discussion with the client.

You may be able to determine which one is effective with some market research of your own.

Understand and manipulate these factors as they affect the particular needs and circumstances of the customer.

The customer will see that a favourable decision is in the customer's own personal favour.

As well as that of the overall fund or company under the customer's control.

ENSURE THE CUSTOMER WORKS WITH YOU AND NO ONE ELSE !

PROPOSITION TO ACTION

You must always finish the argumentation presented to the customer with a proposition to action.

Example:

When would you authorise me to implement this investment portfolio?

How would you authorise me to proceed at this point?

What are your thoughts on the proposition and when would you authorise me to proceed ?

To implement the portfolio call Bill Bloggs on 237 3333.

YOU NOW HAVE THE DEAL !
SELLING SOLUTIONS TO CUSTOMERS IS A NATURAL PROCESS

As you can see, in selling solutions to customers, you must be aware of:

a) **The Customer and the Customer's Customer**

b) **The personal risk of the decision maker**

c) **The Logical Argumentation**

d) **The Proposition to action**

THIS IS HOT RESEARCH / HOT CALLING/HOT BUSINESS

GENERATION OF CORPORATE OPPORTUNITIES

a) Quick BFP (Budget, Functional Proficiency and Prospects) analysis of companies in sector – thumb nail analysis

b) Create broad brush stroke imaginary scenarios for rationalisation of sector

c) Quick think-tank session within the Team to eliminate all or some of scenarios

d) Quickly analyse any surviving scenarios with a view to elimination

e) Quick think-tank session within the Team on surviving scenario/s which pass the BFP test process

f) Arrange think-tank session with Corporate Department to determine corporate potential

g) Pass over to Corporate Department

THE A – Z OF HOT CALLING/MARKETING

A

SELLING OR MARKETING TO A PARTICULAR CUSTOMER

Research the needs of the customer before making contact.

Examine company reports.

Seek advice from the research analysts, other investment professionals etc.

Analyse own customer databases and company records.

Search the library for information.

B

ANALYSING THE EFFECTS

OF YOUR SOLUTIONS

ON THE NEEDS

OF YOUR CUSTOMER

Analyse your solutions for the positive and negative effects the solution has on the budget, function and prospects of the customer.

DEVELOPING THE

ARMOURY

TO WIN THE BATTLE

MORE INITIAL WORK

LEADS TO

GREATER SUCCESS

HOW TO WORK THE SCHEMA

The best research analysts and marketing experts use the following techniques in providing solutions for the customer.

CEO'S / Managing Directors are totally dedicated to and evaluate all your proposed solutions in terms of:

BUDGET

FUNCTION

&

PROSPECTS

As these affect their company.

Your solution must be strong in all or most of these categories.

If not, redesign the solution before marketing.

THE SCHEMA

Analyse your solutions for the positive and negative effects the solution has on the budget, function and prospects of the Customer.

1. **BUDGET** - PROFIT

   - REVENUE

   - EXPENDITURE

COST / BENEFIT ANALYSIS

Determine how the products on offer will increase or decrease the revenue and expenditure of the customer.

The product may have an effect on both revenue and expenditure or only one.

The product may increase expenditure for the customer but more than compensate with the increase in revenue.

As long as the profitability of the customer increases the product is saleable.

If the product does not increase overall customer profitability – rework the product or the explanation of the product so that profitability becomes obvious to the customer.

Sometimes, the product is profitable.

However, the explanation of the product makes the product seem unprofitable.

Revise the explanation.

2. FUNCTIONAL PROFICIENCY
(Administrative Processes)

- Company
- Division
- Sub-Division
- Employee

How will the solutions affect the functional proficiency of a customer at the overall company level and then at the divisional, sub-divisional and individual employee level?

Will the Customer be able to do less administrative work as a result of the solution you are proposing?

If less, the Customer will love you.

The Customer is always looking for solutions which enhance administrative procedures and functional proficiency.

The Customer will be attracted to your solution.

The administrative efficiency of your solution may be the factor which gave you a market advantage over the solutions of your rivals.

These market differentiations earn you the major market share, ahead of your competitors. The demonstrated thoroughness of your approach to the customer is worth money to yourself and your company.

You earn greater bonuses and recognition as experienced Equity Investment/Research experts.

3. **PROSPECTS**
   - **Company**
   - **Division**
   - **Sub-Division**
   - **Employee**

What does your solution do for the customer's business in the short, medium and long term?

Examine the resultant effect of the product on the profitability and business procedures of the customer in the:

**SHORT
MEDIUM
AND
LONG TERM**

Demonstrate to the customer how the customer will be better off, as a result of using your solutions in their business situation.

WORKING WITH THE DECISION MAKERS IN THE CUSTOMER COMPANY

At the senior decision making levels of a company, that is, CEO, board members, fund management selection panels, fund managers, fund analysts and dealers, industry ranking experts, etc, the answers to all of these questions and factors must be known and understood before a decision on the purchase of your solution can be made.

DO THE WORK FOR THE CUSTOMER. THE DEALS WILL FOLLOW.

The customer should simply examine the crushing logic and cost/benefit analysis of your solution to the customer's business needs and agree to the deal.

If the customer has to go away and think about your solution and draw all the conclusions and undertake a cost/benefit analysis based on the data supplied by you, all in the customer's own time, deals are going to be slow in coming.

The customer will appreciate the fact that you are an investment expert who understands the needs of fund/ portfolio managers/financial planners/advisers etc and have the confidence to deal with you now and in the future.

By demonstrating such fund management expertise, you will beat your rivals in the marketplace.

You will pick up those extra market shares from existing customers, move onto more panels, advisor businesses and break into new targets more often.

4. HOW TO DEAL WITH VAGUE FEELS

(What do you do if you have doubts about how the deal is going ?)

In some deals, the research analyst / salesperson has a vague feeling something is not quite right.

Write down the feeling.

Analyse the feeling in terms of budget, function (administrative procedures) and prospects.

The problem will usually fall within one or two of these factors and can then be dealt with clearly.

SUMMARY SCHEMA

Here is the schema for analysing the effects of your products on the needs of the customer's company:

1) Budget

- Profit

- Revenue

- Expenditure

2) Functional Proficiency

- Company
  (Administrative Processes)

- Division

- Sub-Division

- Employee

3) Prospects

- Company

- Division

- Sub-Division

- Employee

4) Dealing with vague feelings

- Analyse in terms of the above-mentioned categories

Marshal McMahon

C

AIDS FOR THE

THOROUGH DEVELOPMENT

OF THE SCHEMA

How to develop a really superb case for the customer to adopt your solution

Marshal McMahon

1

ARISTOTLE'S CATEGORIES OF REALITY = SUPERB ANALYSIS

For an extremely thorough analysis of the previously mentioned Categories of Budget, Function (Administrative Functionality / Functional Proficiency) and Prospects, the following questioning can be applied to the categories:

CATEGORIES   QUESTIONS
                (+ve, -ve effects)

Essence   What is nature of project? What exactly are you aiming to accomplish?

Quality   How good, bad or indifferent is the project or solution in relation to the existing customer position?

Quantity   How many? Does the customer want more, less, or the same of the solution you are offering?

Time   When? Implementation stages, start, conclusion.

Location   Where? What are the effects upon the spatial requirements of customer? More, less, the

Marshal McMahon

same ? Local area, Regional, State, National, International ?

2

OPEN-ENDED QUESTIONS

Open-ended questions demand full answers from the customer and therefore supply maximum information about the customer which can be used to satisfy the needs of the customer.

Closed questions receive yes or no as the answer, you are still in the dark.

Marshal McMahon

OPEN-ENDED QUESTIONS FOR EXTRACTING MAXIMUM INFORMATION FROM CUSTOMERS

All opened – questions demand detailed answers and begin with the following words:

HOW ?

WHEN ?

WHERE ?

WHY ?

WHAT ?

WHICH ?

WHO?

OPEN – ENDED QUESTIONS

Examples:

What are your thoughts on the portfolio re-arrangements ?
Full answer required ?

As opposed to: Do you think the portfolio re-arrangement is a good or a bad one?
Answer: It's OK

When would you authorise me to proceed with the solution ?

How do you wish to proceed with this factor ?

How are you feeling ? Answer must be considered and answered in full.

As opposed to: Are you feeling well ? Answer: yes or no !

Marshal McMahon

D

LOGICAL ARGUMENTATION AND FALL-BACK POSITIONS

COST / BENEFIT ANALYSIS

Analyse and develop logical, business argumentation specifically suited for presentation to the customer.

DEVELOP THE LOGICAL BUSINESS ARGUMENTATION ALONG THE LINES OF BUDGET, FUNCTION (ADMINISTRATIVE EFFICIENCY) AND PROSPECTS

The development of the logical argumentation would be based on the answers to the questioning processes undertaken in relation to the particular project.

The following 3 pages are real life examples of the questioning process.

PRACTICAL EXAMPLE OF QUESTIONING PROCESSES

Here are examples of the questioning process in the development of the sale of a product or portfolio to a customer.

QUESTIONS ON:

BUDGET

1. What is the average loss on a transaction by a customer ?

2. How often do losses occur ?

3. What is the average loss per year ?

4. What is the average, commission cost to the customer ?

5. What steps does your company currently take to facilitate the implementation of the portfolio arrangement ?

6. How can this be amalgamated with the customer's normal procedures, so that your company is seen to be automatically protecting their valued customers ?

7. What are the likely savings on expenditure for each customer ?

8. What are the likely increases in revenue as a result of using your company's equity research expertise for each customer?

FUNCTION

9. What processes does the customer currently undertake in order to gain the benefits of your portfolio solution ?

10. How can these be facilitated, automated ?

11. What is the current logical argumentation convincing the customer to use the system ?

12. What are the propositions placed before the customer evoking action from the customer ?

13. What are the fall-back positions available, if the customer rejects the deal ?

14. What method do you currently use to discover the exact needs of the customer ? Open ended questions versus closed questions.

15. What form of customer database is used ?

PROSPECTS

16. Where in terms of the combined effect of budget and administrative efficiency will the customer be in the short, medium and long term as a result of using your research/fund management skills ?

17. Give examples of cost/benefit analyses of customers using the system compared to those without your research skills.

18. Why are the customers not using the system ?

    Cover budget, function, prospects.

MAIN ARGUMENTATION AND

FALLBACK POSITIONS

As the likelihood that your main argumentation to be presented to the customer covers all the possibilities within the customer's company is remote, as you are not privy to all the happenings and plans within the company, fall-back positions must be prepared.

These fall-back positions logically cover imagined alternative customer, company scenarios.

WHY IS ALL THIS WORK SO VITAL ?

By developing this total marketing approach, you have established yourself and your company to be in a class above the rest of the marketplace.

Demonstrating total dedication to the fundamental business needs of your customers and their customers is the strongest form of marketing possible.

BEAT YOUR COMPETITORS

ESTABLISH MARKET ADVANTAGE AND DIFFERENTIATION

YOUR OWN REMUNERATION, FUNCTIONAL SATISFACTION AND PROSPECTS WILL BE ENHANCED AS A RESULT OF YOUR SUCCESS.

E

DEVELOP THE CUSTOMER'S PERSONAL COMMITMENT TO THE PURCHASE OF THE SOLUTION

Research the persons to be contacted in target company (Rapport).

Analyse the customer in terms of the following factors:

REMUNERATION

FUNCTIONAL SATISFACTION

PROSPECTS

AND LOCATION

Establish which of the personal factors will move the person or potential customer to become committed to concluding the deal.

Each person is personally and primarily concerned with only one or two of these factors. Once you can determine which of these factors is of most concern to the customer, you can angle your argumentation to appeal to that factor within the customer.

Once the customer can see personal maximisation of their driving force from the purchase of the solutions, the customer will become committed to the deal and drive the deal through the required stages to completion.

Knowledge of the customer's personal needs is gained by the use of open-ended questions and the posing of various scenarios concerning the above mentioned factors and watching the responses.

REMUNERATION ORIENTATION

For example, if the customer is remuneration oriented, the customer will become quite interested in the fact that significant bonuses will accrue at the end of the year as a result of the extra profit produced by your solutions.

PROSPECTS ORIENTATION

If the customer is prospects oriented, the customer may not move when bonuses are mentioned.

So mention, how, whoever takes these solutions on board will be famous and must be heading for CEO.

The prospects oriented customer will come to life.

Use your skills to determine which factor or factors are of primary concern to your customer.

USE THE KNOWLEDGE TO DRIVE THE DEAL

F

THE ACTUAL APPROACH

TO THE CUSTOMER

Develop the overall strategy for telephone call or meeting

Here is an example of the sales or marketing approach which could be developed in preparation for the client meeting.

1. Congratulations to customer on excellent results.

2. How is the fund, financial planner/advisor going in these difficult times ?

3. What did you think of the Acme episode ?

4. What do you think of the recent developments in the legal sphere concerning the burden of responsibility for the efficient running of a fund management group/financial planning business or investment fund/company ?

5. The question is: Who is legally responsible for the efficient running of the investment portfolio? The advisor, the dealer group, fund manager, the trustee company, the directors of the company who run the fund ?

Following recent developments, e.g. FSRA, IMA's, Tech crash, building society crashes, etc, investors are determined to hold someone legally responsible for the efficient management of their funds.

Bill, we did well on that last deal. What are your requirements today ?

What did you think of the announcement from the Reserve Bank today ?

How does that affect your requirements ?

I have discussed that with our head of research and we are convinced that you would increase your profit in the following ways by moving out of Acme and using BHP instead.

Then when the Reserve Bank is forced to adjust its strategy in 2 days time, as a result of the war in the Middle East, then we could move out of X shares and lock in the client profit.

You/client should make about $X,000 profit in 2 days. How does that fit in with your current strategy ?

I can arrange to put through the deal at a competitive rate right now, do you authorise me to proceed ?
The deal is through.
By the way, I noticed Tigers lost on Saturday. Those guys are never going to make the finals.

You will have to start backing the best team, St George, mate, the only team.

I have some interesting developments occurring on the Australian equity front at the moment, could be some excellent profit involved, I will call you as soon as I have confirmed the reports.

I should have confirmation around 2pm today. I will give you a call as soon as I know.

Where else can I assist you at the moment ? More research, data on the USA market, etc ?

NO MATTER WHAT HAPPENS AT THE

MEETING YOU ARE NOW PREPARED

TO RUN THE MEETING ALONG

THESE LINES.

BE FLEXIBLE, THE CLIENT
MAY HAVE

OTHER IDEAS AT THE
MEETING.

RUN
WITH THE CLIENT AND

MAKE SURE

YOUR POINTS ARE ALSO
COVERED

THROUGHOUT THE
MEETING, EVEN IF
IN A MODIFIED FORM.

Marshal McMahon

G

PROPOSITIONS TO ACTION

Develop a proposition

To be placed to the customer

Which will close the deal

PROPOSITIONS

CLOSE

DEALS

IF YOU PUT THE PROPOSITION AFTER

ALL YOUR HARD WORK, YOU WILL

MAKE 9 OUT OF 10 DEALS.

IF YOU DO ALL THE REST OF THE WORK

AND MISS THE PROPOSITION, YOU

WILL LOSE HALF THE DEALS.

After the argumentation, the customer needs to be directed to a decision by a proposition to action.

The customer is expecting you to guide the customer to the completion of the deal.

You are making the deal.
The customer expects that you will begin and end the whole process.

In fact, if you forget to make the proposition and close the deal, the customer is left wondering if you know what you are doing.

Your expertise is in question.

Be an expert. Close the deals. Use the proposition.

If the proposition to action is forgotten, the deal may fall away through in-activity, just when everything seemed to be going well.

The customer expects to be propositioned by the proposer of the deal.

At that point the customer gives a considered decision on how to proceed.

THE AIM OF THE PROPOSITION IS TO OBTAIN ONE OF THE FOLLOWING ANSWERS:

YES

NO or

MAYBE

"**YES**" is the best.

"**NO**" or "**MAYBE**" are the next best and lead to deals.

Find out what is causing the problem and solve the problem.

Once the problem is determined and solved, the sale will almost certainly proceed.

If you have prepared well, you will probably find that the customer missed some vital point in the presentation which when re-presented will clarify the problem and lead to a sale.

Here are some examples of propositions which can be placed before a customer:

PROPOSITIONS TO FACILITATE DECISIONS BY CLIENTS RE DEALS

1. To implement this portfolio, call Bill Blogg on 237 3333.

    1.1 I could give you a discounted rate on this portfolio right now. If you implemented this portfolio at this rate that should give the client and you increased profits of \$X,000 and \$Y,000 over the next year, that's an excellent profit, would you like me to proceed with the order, Bill ?

    1.2 What would you authorise me to do at this stage ?

2. How do you authorise me to proceed at this point ?

3. What are your thoughts on the proposition and when do you authorise me to proceed ?

4. What would you authorise me to do in relation to the deal ? e.g. research, market information, options ?

5. At what rate/price or point, would you authorise the purchase (or sale) of the investment product ? If I can arrange to a deal at that rate, would you authorise me to proceed ?

6. When do you authorise me to proceed with the deal ?

7. What aspect of the deal concerns you at this stage ? State the problem will be solved. Then ask at what quantity, when and at what price the customer would want to buy the product.

8. Where does this deal fit in your overall portfolio strategy ? . . . if that is the case, when do you authorise me to proceed with the deal ?

9. What are the problems in this deal ?
10. What are the problems in this market as seen by your organisation ?

11. If not this deal, what are you currently seeking in your portfolio balance ? . . . if I

could arrange that balance would you authorise me to proceed with an order or the deal ?

12. Where else can I assist you at the moment ? e.g. Research, protection, etc ?

13. Why not let our company provide you with that
information ?

14. You have read the research. What are your thoughts on such and such a point ?

15. What direction are you aiming at in the short term ? Medium term ? Long term ?

16. What time would suit you best for the execution of the investment order or deal ?

17. What else do you need to know about the deal ? Research market movements, options ?

18. I am targeting my client's needs and focusing my efforts to more accurately assist you, what is your overall investment philosophy ?

19. Our company is giving a presentation on your leading investment strategies, funds, stocks, etc. Would November 30 be suitable ? If not, what time would suit you and your planners ?

H

PRESENTATIONS

Voice
- Turkey Stretch for larynx and throat muscles (5 minutes)
- Force your larynx further and further down the throat
- Creates deep, rich voice tone – creates impact and credibility

Diaphragm Stretches
- 6 deep breaths and hold for 10 seconds each
- space well to prevent giddiness

Speed of Delivery
- the larger the group the slower you deliver
- maximises hearing and understanding by listeners
- Practice with a friend at end of auditorium

Delivery method
- read ahead 3 words at a time then face audience and deliver

Overheads
- maximum of 3 by 1 line per slide
- for maximum impact 1 word or line per slide is best

Z

CUSTOMER DATABASES

As the human brain will recall only 2% of the data collected about a customer within 24 hours, you must record the data on a customer data system. The system can be either on computer or cards.

Here is a suggested CUSTOMER DATA SYSTEM

CUSTOMER DATA SYSTEM

CONTACT
Customer Class: A, B, C

A=major product buyer

B=minor product buyer

C=communicates

NAME	:
AGE	:
ADDRESS	:
BUSINESS	:
HOME	:

EDUCATION
UNIVERSITY, ETC

QUALIFICATIONS	:
FAMILY	:
WIFE	:
CHILDREN	:
SCHOOLS	:
AGES	:
CLUBS, SPORTS, HOBBIES	:

INHOUSE CONTACTS:
1)
2)
3)

OPERATING PHILOSOPHY:

BUDGET?
FUNCTION?
PROSPECTS?

(Short – Medium – Long term Scenarios)

| STOCKS HELD | : | MAJOR |
| | : | MINOR |

| STOCKS | : | ACTIVE |
| | : | IN-ACTIVE |

| STOCKS TRADED | : | |

| LAST PURCHASES /SALES | : | |

LUNCHEONS   :

PRESENTATIONS   :

CUSTOMER VISITS   :

CUSTOMER ENTERTAINMENT   :
CUSTOMER'S PERSONAL AIMS:

    1) PROSPECTS
    2) FUNCTIONAL SATISFACTION
    3) REMUNERATION
    4) LOCATION

CUSTOMER'S ATTITUDE TO YOUR COMPANY'S ABILITIES:

1) RESEARCH
2) EXECUTION
3) PORTFOLIO PERFORMANCE
4) MARKETING
5) PRODUCT RANGE
6) PRODUCT DEVELOPMENT
7) BRAND

Hot Research – Hot Calling –

Hot Business Results

Nearly 2000 people have attended the Hot Calling/ Hot Research/Hot Business Courses over the years.

Many people have gone onto good success in their lives and business using the Hot Business Principles.

From this initial group quite a few quickly or gradually went on to become highly ranked analysts or business people.

In that initial group, not one analyst was able to give more than 1 of the fundamental factors that comprised a company.

Most got Finance or Budget as a fundamental element of a company.

A few got Function as an essential element of a company.

But none of the highly paid analysts got all 3.

However, there were 2 young women who attended the course that day.

Both of them were secretaries to the highly paid analysts.

Both rattled off all 3 elements in quick succession:

Budget – Function – Prospects

The analysts were shocked and thought that somehow the 2 secretaries had been primed beforehand.

The young women and I denied any prompting had taken place.

Many of the analysts argued that no one would know all 3 immediately.

The secretaries were a fluke.

Many of the analysts did not accept my observation that every CEO would know all 3 elements immediately.

At the time of this heated argument, the CEO of the whole merchant bank came into the room to see how the course was going.

OK. Ask the CEO the big question.

So I asked the CEO what would be the fundamental elements of a company?

In 1 second he said: Budgetary, Functional matters and the Prospect for the company – especially taking into account the first 2 elements.

You could have heard a pin drop in the room.

The CEO then asked how the analyst group had faired on this question.

I replied that not 1 analyst had known all 3 elements.

But that the 2 young secretaries had given the answer in quick time.

The CEO congratulated the 2 secretaries.

He said a few choice words for the analysts and left the room.

I had been arguing that PROSPECTS was the most important element of a company.

The analysts had disagreed focusing on FINANCE.

So I asked the CEO just before he left the room – which was the most important?

PROSPECTS was the reply.

Immediately following the course I started working with the analysts on improving their logical analysis of companies and their marketing skills.

At the time, there were no highly ranked analysts in the group.

By the end of the year, there were about 1-3 top 3 ranked analysts with quite a few more in the top 10 ranked analysts.

The company was starting to make profit.

One of the analysts was immediately able to think of long range corporate possibilities for a company.

He wrote a report on how the company could expand over time.

The report was passed to the corporate finance division who succeeded in converting the ideas to action plans.

More profit for the bank.

Another analyst created a masterpiece on how a particular company could grow and increase profitability.

He showed a draft of his ideas to the company.

The company flew him to their head office.

They were astonished by his logical analysis.

With the publication of the report to the fund managers, he became number 1 ranked analyst in that field.

Sometime later, the analyst was offered a position with the company concerned that he could not refuse.

The next Hot Calling course was for the dealing or sales desk.

The dealers were split between the red wine brigade and those searching for a better way to do business.

I was really looking forwards to the fray.

I knew that there would be great debate or rather attempted put down by the red wine brigade.

What a course.

Almost no one got the fundamentals of a company right.

A few loved the logical way of doing business with the clients and the potential ways to gain some knew clients.

The red wine brigade vowed to spend even more on the lunches.

After all these years why change.

I suggested that soon the underperforming sales persons would develop into mature business people who would succeed in opening up new accounts and increasing profitability for the bank.

Rubbish said the red wine masters.

In a few months the new way sales staff started kicking goals.

Some of the kicks were significant.

The red winers started looking like underperformers.

The new way sales staff started gaining power through successful deals.

There was one mild mannered dealer/salesman who was the stated enemy of the red winers.

He was always on the outer with the red winers.

Now he was making deals of size and breaking into top clients.

The red winers had been trying to break into one of the biggest potential clients in town for years without success.

In fact, the potential client stated that they may never do business with us.

The mild mannered dealer was eternally asking to be given the account.

He would service them with logical analysis and marketing techniques.

Finally, the account was given to the mild one for a go.

I think that soon after the first call to the potential big client, the mild one made his first order.

And on he went becoming a team leader and eventually a highly ranked member of the bank.

Some of the red winers converted.

Others went to other companies or divisions of the bank.

Some employees I worked with did not realise that they were on their final chance.

If they did not come good in 2-3 weeks, they would be asked to leave.

I never use the word fire so I asked that I focus on them solidly for 2-3 weeks before a decision was made by others.

I am happy to say that all came good and went onto solid careers.

I was amused when years later, they claimed my work with them was a waste of time.

Little do they know.

Others realised what was going on at the time.

I keep quiet.

Marshal McMahon

I prefer subvision.

A few people have worked out my subvision style over the years.

Most people think they are doing it all by themselves.

I am not a teacher, I hope.

I try to be an educator (e-duco: I lead out of).

There are volumes to be written about banking and finance.

But that will have to wait for a future novel.

After 5 years at the bank, an opportunity arose to be part of a product development business.

Now I learnt a lot more about business.

The business group were honourable and successful in their own right.

I was privileged to be part of such an ethical business.

Their word was absolute.

The initial phase was a challenge.

Finding suitable manufacturers and researchers to develop the new concept.

To my surprise, I found that companies large and small from all around the world were initially cooperative.

They are always looking for new outlets for their production base.

However, almost no company had the skills to develop and test the prototypes.

Eventually, a small company in Europe understood over the phone what needed to be done and sent me a sample of their skill base.

They were smart and inventive.

Our business agreed to work with them to develop prototypes.

This small company had logical engineering minds and ethics.

Their researchers had the skill to develop prototypes at a fast pace.

To test the prototypes we linked with a nearby university which had a highly skilled engineering department.

The head of the department was logical and ethical.

He understood the project immediately.

His testing facility validated the performances of our new product.

So we had proven the concept.

Next, step was to approach a manufacturer in the area of our product with the aim of licensing them to produce and distribute the product.

Lesson 1: big companies are only too happy to talk with you and say they want the product.

Lesson 2: as long as you spend more of your own money to advance the product just a little bit more

Lesson 3: their engineering departments can be blinkered by their own interests

Lesson 4: the logical engineers in their group will bow to the illogic of the senior engineers – even though they know the truth of the matter

Lesson 5: they will try to drag out all negotiations till you run out of money

Lesson 6: they will offer a pittance to take the product off your hands when you have run low on money

Lesson 7: heads of companies are frightened to sign a contract with you in case all fails and they wear the consequences – like demotion or dismissal

Lesson 8: heads of companies can be frightened to make decisions even if their own market research shows overwhelming support for the product in blind testing

Lesson 9: soon after losing the opportunity for your product, their company will produce new product which their engineering department says is great.

Lesson 10: their new developments usually fail badly

Lesson 11: prefer trade secrets over patenting

Lesson 12: never reveal all in a patent – keep some key element a secret

Lesson 13: the big guys with money love working from other companies' patents

Engineering Departments

On one occasion, the head engineer was espousing how the principles of the industry really worked.

He was completely wrong engineeringly.

There were about 7 engineers in his group.

All agreed with him.

Our company explained how the engineering principles really worked.

Our engineer was at the meeting.

Plus I used logic.

All his engineers looked most uncomfortable.

They could see that their head engineer was wrong.

But they were frightened to speak up in case they lost their jobs.

Then one new engineer with their firm spoke up and said that he could not sit there and deny proven engineering principles.

He was on the side of truth and justice.

The head engineer left the meeting.

Marshal McMahon

The young guy told us at the end of the meeting he would rather work elsewhere than deny reality.

He left the company soon after.

The head engineer advised his corporate bosses that our product engineering was all wrong.

We showed the corporate bosses the truth of the matter.

But they were too frightened to countermand the head engineer's opinions.

He was a forceful engineer.

So untruth reigned.

In apparent desperation, this company came out with several poor new products which were unsuccessful.

I would rather go surfing than live a lie.

Not long after these episodes, the senior management of the company underwent changes.

Another major company stated that they wanted the product.

So we had a meeting with their engineering department.

The head engineer challenged our engineering principles in another area.

He was wrong.

So we proved the engineering principles.

His engineers looked embarrassed by the discussion.

But again they kept quiet.

The head engineer demanded that he was right.

Aristotle would have loved his Argumentum ad Hominem and Argument from Authority.

Of course, within a few months, that company had a new racquet on the market using the principles from the discussion.

Only trouble was: the claims related to the new model were wrong.

He had not understood what the engineering principle really meant.

My associates and I understood that most minds do not think logically even at head engineer level in our product field.

Aristotle distinguished between the types of argumentation and brains over 2000 years ago.

Nothing has changed.

That I can see.

The world of politics may be another shining example of the different types of brains.

Several large companies were enthusiastic to have our product.

Yet the moment, we chose one company, the major rival wrote us a letter advising that we were now the enemy and that they would conduct themselves appropriately.

Within a short period of time, one of our associates received a letter from that losing company advising that if he did not leave our company immediately his contract with them would be cancelled.

We understood that our associate needed to stay with this threatening company.

The losing company conducted a worldwide negative campaign concerning our product before it even hit the market place.

The corporate world is a lovely place.

Reflects the fear and greed of some humans.

The cost of developing and manufacturing our product to market was low.

Yet, as a bargaining tool, the major companies exaggerate the cost enormously.

Unfortunately, our company trusted to some degree, the words of the company that we were negotiating with for a contract to develop and market our product.

If I had my time again, I would not take any company at their word and stick to the deadlines agreed.

Call the deal off if the first deadline is missed no matter what the excuse.

The company is probably dragging out negotiations till you go broke.

Then they will offer you a pittance to take the mess off your hands.

The product then goes either of 2 ways:

- either into the bottom draw never to be seen or
- developed at a time to suit them

Once their lawyers take over the negotiations and the management pulls back refusing to take your calls and contacts – consider moving elsewhere or developing the product another way.

A 1 month deadline to sign the contract passed with promises that it would be a few weeks.

18 months of promises later we ceased negotiations.

One of the sticking points at the interested parties end was: who was going to sign the contract with us at their end.

The CEO dumped the signing onto the GM.

The GM lived in fear of being blamed if all went wrong and argued that the CEO should sign.

Fear of failure ruled.

The day we advised that the contract must be signed by 5pm that day, panic broke out at the major company.

The company rang at 2 minutes to 5 and asked for the weekend.

They would sign on Monday.

We argued that they had 2 minutes left.

Panic at their end.

I will call you back in a few minutes.

Sorry times up.

I will talk to our management and call you back.

Never got a call back.

Surprise.

There was fear to sign even though their world market testing showed that around 90% of players chose our product in blind player tests.

At one point, the management argued that this was not a great result.

Some companies bring out new products on a 10% market approval rating.

Some political parties will go to an election on a 1-2% swing to their party.

Did not want the product.

Too much personal risk.

The same company brought out a new range of improved products soon after losing our product.

All of which failed ignominiously.

Surprise – the senior management started taking up positions at other companies.

If you can, develop the product yourself.

If you are successful, the big guys are greedy enough to buy you out.

I can understand that big profitable companies reduce their risk taking by leaving the risk to small companies.

If the small companies are successful, the large company has the cash flow to buy out the little guy.

But if the big company is struggling and cash poor, they should take their lives in their hands and spend a pittance on developing new products.

However, fear of failure in a failing company is a major issue.

Only the strong can make logical decisions in these circumstances.

Our company then developed a retrofit kit which worked on most market products.

We sold a few thousand units in the market place.

Then decided to appoint a distributor in one of the largest world market places.

The interviews went well with potential distributors, especially the one of the biggest product distributors.

We came to a deal with that distributor.

Product was sent.

Weeks went by.

I received a call from one of our keenest product users in that market place.

Marshal McMahon

He had been to a trade fair to check out the new products.

He attended the presentation of our product by our distributor.

The distributor ran our product down strongly.

Our keen user was so disgusted at the lies that he spoke up at the presentation.

Pointing out the misrepresentations about our product.

The presentation was quite disturbing.

Our user was a highly ranked player and a logical engineer.

He contacted me immediately to advise that I needed a new distributor.

I contacted the distributor.

The distributor said: well that's the way we see it.

Why did you take on the product in the first place?

No answer.

We cancelled the deal.

Collusion in the market place at high levels may be a factor.

Some countries have an appetite for the new and logical.

There is a logical culture in some places.

Fear and greed rules in most places it would appear.

We developed a retro fit version of our product so that the major potential buyers of our product would not feel threatened and still be willing to negotiate with us.

If I had my time over, I would have made the full product from the beginning.

Why did we not now make the full version ourselves?

Well, the company had little money left and then came a major worldwide financial crisis.

That was the end of the project.

I could make the product now – but the cost of marketing would be a major issue.

The opposing forces would conduct strong negative campaigns against any new product launch.

During the development phase of the new product business, we dealt with some of the world's top advisory firms.

Most are keen that you set yourself up correctly from the start.

Particularly, the use of tax havens.

If I could say one thing about tax havens after some limited experience, it would be to pay tax in your country of choice.

Lifestyle and happiness is more important than living in a tax haven in the hope that one day you will be rich and famous.

Most tax havens have a pleasant initial appeal.

This lasts for about 3 days.

Then life in a golden prison takes over.

If life was a golden prison there, then most people would live there.

Most people use the tax haven as a post box.

Living somewhere else.

Go for your own happiness first in life.

You only live once.

The degree of unhappiness in some tax havens is indirectly proportional to the amount of money earned.

Greed and fear can really take hold there.

Some people tortured themselves with the fact that their neighbour had 1 billion more than they did.

Even if they had billions themselves.

How unhappy can you be.

Then there were the gold diggers.

People who were prepared to marry money just for the divorce 8-12 months later.

What a game.

Prenups became the name of the game around that time.

Gold digging seemed to reduce a little.

Affairs – well.

Business trips – well.

Expensive cars.

I did have a long drive in a top sports car with the muffler hotted up.

Hot Business

After 1-2 hours the pain was numbed by more pain.

One day poetry in motion went passed.

We were driving down a very narrow and winding road by the sea.

I saw a motor cycle about 1 km behind me.

I looked again a few seconds later.

The motor bike sailed past us and disappeared into the winding distance in seconds.

The leaning on the cornering was pure poetry.

Then I remembered the number plate.

A previous number 1 Grand Prix rider.

How beautiful.

But remember, others, that he had perfected his skills over a long period of time.

Most people would have been dead riding the coast road at that speed.

Another factor of some people living the tax haven dream is that they are superior in all matters.

I could not believe that some people really thought they had a chance of beating you at a game in which you were a professional.

In fact, after each game they were full of powerful reasons on why you had beaten them.

Marshal McMahon

Somehow I was just lucky.

But I had seen this in London when coaching at high level.

Some top 10 players would let some rich person get close to them in a friendly game.

Afterwards, the rich person would go around boasting how they nearly beat one of the best in the world.

Dream on.

Some people live in a world of their own glory.

Convinced they are near the top in many fields.

And would be the top if only they dedicated themselves to that field.

There were other projects which again reflected the same lessons around this time.

But they may be part of another in principle novel.

Upon returning to our home country, I was asked to develop a Hot Education Course for high school students.

Hot Education is part of Sit on a Hot Pot or is now available as a separate book.

Marshal McMahon